THE PROMISE
PRINCIPLE JOURNAL

Belongs To: _____

From Date: _____ To Date: _____

THE PROMISE PRINCIPLE JOURNAL

PHILLIP HUNTER

Affirmation and a spirit of unity provide the perfect setting for the Holy Spirit to work powerfully in the hearts of the people in your group.

–Phillip Hunter

My Index

Page	Date	Scripture	Promise
....	....	....	....
....	....	....	....
....	....	....	....
....	....	....	....
....	....	....	....
....	....	....	....
....	....	....	....
....	....	....	....
....	....	....	....
....	....	....	....
....	....	....	....
....	....	....	....
....	....	....	....
....	....	....	....
....	....	....	....
....	....	....	....
....	....	....	....
....	....	....	....

Page	Date	Scripture	Promise
....	....	....	....
....	....	....	....
....	....	....	....
....	....	....	....
....	....	....	....
....	....	....	....
....	....	....	....
....	....	....	....
....	....	....	....
....	....	....	....
....	....	....	....
....	....	....	....
....	....	....	....
....	....	....	....
....	....	....	....
....	....	....	....
....	....	....	....
....	....	....	....
....	....	....	....
....	....	....	....
....	....	....	....
....	....	....	....
....	....	....	....

Study Technique

The *Promise Principle*™ is based on 2 Peter 1:3–11. God has given us His promises to participate in His nature rather than live in our nature. Our nature is to be ruled by our circumstances.

In view of all this, make every effort to respond to God's promises (2 Peter 1:5).

How can I identify God's promises?

His promises are either a truth or a commandment.

How do I respond to God's promises?

1. Ask by faith (Matthew 21:22; James 4:2b)
2. Receive with thanks (1 Timothy 4:4; Ephesians 5:20)

Every truth and commandment is a promise from God. As you read, underline every promise from God and ask yourself if this is a promise you should ask God for in faith or receive with a thankful heart. Then pray it!

Pray about everything (Philippians 4:6).

Example #1 from Ephesians

God decided in advance to adopt us into his own family by bringing us to himself through Jesus Christ. This is what he wanted to do, and it gave him great pleasure (Ephesians 1:5).

Is this a promise you should ask for in faith or receive with thanks?

Receive with thanks!

Ask the Holy Spirit how you need to respond to this promise based on the circumstances in your life. Then pray it.

Lord, there are times when I feel unloved and struggle with loneliness, but I thank you that you picked me and made me a part of your family. I am loved by you. I belong! Thank you that you desire me, Amen.

Example #2 from Ephesians

Asking God, the glorious Father of our Lord Jesus Christ, to give you spiritual wisdom and insight so that you might grow in your knowledge of God. I pray that your hearts will be flooded with light so that you can understand the confident hope he has given to those he called—his holy people who are his rich and glorious inheritance (Ephesians 1:17-18).

Is this a promise you should ask for in faith or receive with thanks?

Ask for by faith!

Ask the Holy Spirit how you need to respond to this promise based on the circumstances in your life. Then pray it.

Lord, I want to know you and all that you have for me. I ask you to give me spiritual wisdom and insight. My desire is to grown in my knowledge of you. I need to know you because I feel despair, I am anxious, I am filled with fear Would you fill my heart with light and overcome the darkness? Help me to understand the hope that I have in you. I want you to be my confidence, Amen.

Recap

1. Underline the promises as you read.
2. Identify the promise as a truth or a commandment.
3. Ask the Holy Spirit what circumstance in your life is touched by this promise.
4. Do you need to ask, do you need to receive it, or both?
5. Pray it!
6. Journal what the Holy Spirit is saying to you.

Promise Principle Group Guide

The group facilitator's job is not to teach the students, but to shepherd the group through God's Word. A good shepherd cares for those God has entrusted to him or her. Remember this as you facilitate the group with C.A.R.E. as your guiding acronym.

Connect (with God)

Begin your group with prayer, thanking God for these participants and asking Him to meet with you. "Teach us as we respond to all that you have for us." (2 minutes.)

Aim

We always want to point the group to the *Promise Principle*. The apostle Peter tells us we have all we need to live as godly people (2 Peter 1:3–4). God has given us all these promises; if we respond to them, it will add to our faith, it will allow us to be productive in our knowledge, and we can participate in His nature rather than our own sinful nature. So we respond to each promise by *receiving it with thanks or asking for it by faith!* (3 minutes.)

Respond (to the Word)

Each week, read one chapter aloud from a selected book of the Bible. Have each person read the next verse as you go around the circle. I recommend doing this so that every person is engaged in Scripture. However, be sensitive to those who cannot read or have great difficulty reading aloud. The goal is to engage, not to embarrass.

Have the members of the group underline every promise. When a person points out a promise, as the facilitator, ask if this is a promise *for which we should thank God* or one *which we should ask Him for by faith.* Then ask the person to share why this truth or commandment is something that requires a response. This practice allows the person to interact with Scripture at a heart level rather than just a head level. Then ask that person to take what has just been verbalized and pray it.

Through this format, people will be able to be vulnerable with things that are occurring in their lives; the Holy Spirit,

God's Word, and other people in the group can minister to them. (45 minutes.)

The Holy Spirit will teach your group as members are praying or as they listen to one another. Ask the group to write down promises or truths the Holy Spirit speaks to them about during the study. God spoke these promises to them, and we want them to remember these promises and continue to pray them out in their lives. (5 minutes.)

Encourage

Encourage the group to continue in the Bible book you are studying and go through a chapter every day. They should underline promises or truths that they find and ask the Lord whether these are promises that they should ask for by faith or something that they should receive with thanks. We encourage the group to invite friends, telling them that they can just listen the first time. We really want the atmosphere of the entire hour to be filled with affirmation. Affirmation and a spirit of unity provide the perfect setting for the Holy Spirit to work powerfully in the hearts of the people in your group. (5 minutes.)

Coaching Tips for the Study

- When a group member explains an underlined truth or promise, let that person talk about it for a moment—that is how to process with the mind. Then ask the member how they should respond to that truth. We are teaching people how to engage their spirit with the Lord. This is where the truth becomes not merely information but leads to transformation.

- Sometimes you will need to press a little bit and ask your members if they are dealing with specific circumstances that they need to pray about or respond to with promises. You must help them and may need to lead with transparency in your own life.

- Engage those who don't talk. They are processing the whole time, and you need to give them space to verbalize these things. I will usually ask them near the end if a particular verse spoke to them. I will then encourage them to respond to it.

- Always give credit to the Holy Spirit whenever someone learns something. We are teaching them that the Holy Spirit is the one who guides us into all truth. The Spirit reveals much in God's Word through discussion and prayer. When something jumps up in a person's spirit so that the person thinks, "Oh, that is good," reinforce the understanding that the Holy Spirit spoke to this person's heart. Make sure the group member writes it down. I always say, "A dull pencil is better than the sharpest mind at recording the whispers of God."

- Allow your members to minister to one another. Many times a person will see something in Scripture that applies to someone else's circumstance. Let them pray for each other.

EXAMPLE

DATE: 3/23/2017   SCRIPTURE: I Peter 5

PROMISE:
vs. 10 In his kindness God called you to share in his eternal glory by means of Christ Jesus. So after you have suffered a little while, he will restore, support, and strengthen you, and he will place you on a firm foundation. —truth

CIRCUMSTANCE:
The past two years I have been struggling through the loss of my marriage. I have been seeking the Lord, but

I feel like this season of grief and loneliness is never going to end. I am wanting to do it the Lord's way, and trusting his promise that he will restore me, that he is strengthening me, and that he has a future that is secure for me...

RESPONSE:
Dear Heavenly Father, I come to you right now and praise you for your faithfulness. Thank you that you see me and know exactly what I am going through. Lord, I confess that I am discouraged and struggle with wondering if this season will end. I receive your promise that you support me and strengthen me. Thank you for restoring my soul and I thank you in advance for putting me on a firm foundation. I love you, Amen.

DATE: ....   SCRIPTURE: ....

PROMISE:

....

....

CIRCUMSTANCE:

....

....

....

RESPONSE:

....

....

....

....

....

DATE: ....   SCRIPTURE: ....

PROMISE:

....

....

CIRCUMSTANCE:

....

....

....

RESPONSE:

....

....

....

....

....

DATE: .... SCRIPTURE: ....

PROMISE:

....

....

CIRCUMSTANCE:

....

....

....

RESPONSE:

....

....

....

....

....

DATE: .... SCRIPTURE: ....

PROMISE:

....

....

CIRCUMSTANCE:

....

....

....

RESPONSE:

....

....

....

....

....

DATE: .... SCRIPTURE: ....

PROMISE:

....
....

CIRCUMSTANCE:

....
....
....

RESPONSE:

....
....
....
....
....

DATE: .... SCRIPTURE: ....

PROMISE:

....
....

CIRCUMSTANCE:

....
....
....

RESPONSE:

....
....
....
....
....

DATE: .... SCRIPTURE: ....

PROMISE:

....
....

CIRCUMSTANCE:

....
....
....

RESPONSE:

....
....
....
....
....

DATE: .... SCRIPTURE: ....

PROMISE:

....
....

CIRCUMSTANCE:

....
....
....

RESPONSE:

....
....
....
....
....

DATE: .... SCRIPTURE: ....

PROMISE:

....
....

CIRCUMSTANCE:

....
....
....

RESPONSE:

....
....
....
....
....

DATE: .... SCRIPTURE: ....

PROMISE:

....
....

CIRCUMSTANCE:

....
....
....

RESPONSE:

....
....
....
....
....

DATE: .... SCRIPTURE: ....

PROMISE:

....

....

CIRCUMSTANCE:

....

....

....

RESPONSE:

....

....

....

....

....

DATE: .... SCRIPTURE: ....

PROMISE:

....

....

CIRCUMSTANCE:

....

....

....

RESPONSE:

....

....

....

....

....

DATE: .... SCRIPTURE: ....

PROMISE:

....

....

CIRCUMSTANCE:

....

....

....

RESPONSE:

....

....

....

....

....

DATE: .... SCRIPTURE: ....

PROMISE:

....

....

CIRCUMSTANCE:

....

....

....

RESPONSE:

....

....

....

....

....

DATE: ....   SCRIPTURE: ....

PROMISE:

....

....

CIRCUMSTANCE:

....

....

....

RESPONSE:

....

....

....

....

....

DATE: ....   SCRIPTURE: ....

PROMISE:

....

....

CIRCUMSTANCE:

....

....

....

RESPONSE:

....

....

....

....

....

DATE: .... SCRIPTURE: ....

PROMISE:

....
....

CIRCUMSTANCE:

....
....
....

RESPONSE:

....
....
....
....
....

DATE: .... SCRIPTURE: ....

PROMISE:

....
....

CIRCUMSTANCE:

....
....
....

RESPONSE:

....
....
....
....
....

DATE: .... SCRIPTURE: ....

PROMISE:

....
....

CIRCUMSTANCE:

....
....
....

RESPONSE:

....
....
....
....
....

DATE: .... SCRIPTURE: ....

PROMISE:

....
....

CIRCUMSTANCE:

....
....
....

RESPONSE:

....
....
....
....
....

DATE: .... SCRIPTURE: ....

PROMISE:
....
....

CIRCUMSTANCE:
....
....
....

RESPONSE:
....
....
....
....
....

DATE: .... SCRIPTURE: ....

PROMISE:
....
....

CIRCUMSTANCE:
....
....
....

RESPONSE:
....
....
....
....
....

DATE: ....   SCRIPTURE: ....

PROMISE:

....

....

CIRCUMSTANCE:

....

....

....

RESPONSE:

....

....

....

....

....

DATE: ....   SCRIPTURE: ....

PROMISE:

....

....

CIRCUMSTANCE:

....

....

....

RESPONSE:

....

....

....

....

....

DATE: .... SCRIPTURE: ....

PROMISE:

....

....

CIRCUMSTANCE:

....

....

....

RESPONSE:

....

....

....

....

....

DATE: .... SCRIPTURE: ....

PROMISE:

....

....

CIRCUMSTANCE:

....

....

....

RESPONSE:

....

....

....

....

....

DATE: ....   SCRIPTURE: ....

PROMISE:

....
....

CIRCUMSTANCE:

....
....
....

RESPONSE:

....
....
....
....
....

DATE: ....   SCRIPTURE: ....

PROMISE:

....
....

CIRCUMSTANCE:

....
....
....

RESPONSE:

....
....
....
....
....

DATE: ....   SCRIPTURE: ....
PROMISE:
....
....
CIRCUMSTANCE:
....
....
....
RESPONSE:
....
....
....
....
....

DATE: ....   SCRIPTURE: ....
PROMISE:
....
....
CIRCUMSTANCE:
....
....
....
RESPONSE:
....
....
....
....
....

DATE: .... SCRIPTURE: ....

PROMISE:

....
....

CIRCUMSTANCE:

....
....
....

RESPONSE:

....
....
....
....
....

DATE: .... SCRIPTURE: ....

PROMISE:

....
....

CIRCUMSTANCE:

....
....
....

RESPONSE:

....
....
....
....
....

DATE: ....   SCRIPTURE: ....

PROMISE:

....

....

CIRCUMSTANCE:

....

....

....

RESPONSE:

....

....

....

....

....

DATE: ....   SCRIPTURE: ....

PROMISE:

....

....

CIRCUMSTANCE:

....

....

....

RESPONSE:

....

....

....

....

....

DATE: ....   SCRIPTURE: ....

PROMISE:

....

....

CIRCUMSTANCE:

....

....

....

RESPONSE:

....

....

....

....

....

DATE: ....   SCRIPTURE: ....

PROMISE:

....

....

CIRCUMSTANCE:

....

....

....

RESPONSE:

....

....

....

....

....

DATE: .... SCRIPTURE: ....

PROMISE:

....

....

CIRCUMSTANCE:

....

....

....

RESPONSE:

....

....

....

....

....

DATE: .... SCRIPTURE: ....

PROMISE:

....

....

CIRCUMSTANCE:

....

....

....

RESPONSE:

....

....

....

....

....

DATE: .... SCRIPTURE: ....

PROMISE:

....
....

CIRCUMSTANCE:

....
....
....

RESPONSE:

....
....
....
....
....

DATE: .... SCRIPTURE: ....

PROMISE:

....
....

CIRCUMSTANCE:

....
....
....

RESPONSE:

....
....
....
....
....

DATE: ....   SCRIPTURE: ....

PROMISE:

....

....

CIRCUMSTANCE:

....

....

....

RESPONSE:

....

....

....

....

....

DATE: ....   SCRIPTURE: ....

PROMISE:

....

....

CIRCUMSTANCE:

....

....

....

RESPONSE:

....

....

....

....

....

DATE: ....   SCRIPTURE: ....

PROMISE:

....
....

CIRCUMSTANCE:

....
....
....

RESPONSE:

....
....
....
....
....

DATE: ....   SCRIPTURE: ....

PROMISE:

....
....

CIRCUMSTANCE:

....
....
....

RESPONSE:

....
....
....
....
....

DATE: ....   SCRIPTURE: ....

PROMISE:

....

....

CIRCUMSTANCE:

....

....

....

RESPONSE:

....

....

....

....

....

DATE: ....   SCRIPTURE: ....

PROMISE:

....

....

CIRCUMSTANCE:

....

....

....

RESPONSE:

....

....

....

....

....

DATE: ....   SCRIPTURE:...............................

PROMISE:

....
....

CIRCUMSTANCE:

....
....
....

RESPONSE:

....
....
....
....
....

DATE: ....   SCRIPTURE:...............................

PROMISE:

....
....

CIRCUMSTANCE:

....
....
....

RESPONSE:

....
....
....
....
....

DATE: ....   SCRIPTURE: ....

PROMISE:

....
....

CIRCUMSTANCE:

....
....
....

RESPONSE:

....
....
....
....
....

DATE: ....   SCRIPTURE: ....

PROMISE:

....
....

CIRCUMSTANCE:

....
....
....

RESPONSE:

....
....
....
....
....

DATE: .... SCRIPTURE:................................

PROMISE:

....
....

CIRCUMSTANCE:

....
....
....

RESPONSE:

....
....
....
....
....

DATE: .... SCRIPTURE:................................

PROMISE:

....
....

CIRCUMSTANCE:

....
....
....

RESPONSE:

....
....
....
....
....

DATE: .... SCRIPTURE: ....

PROMISE:

....
....

CIRCUMSTANCE:

....
....
....

RESPONSE:

....
....
....
....
....

DATE: .... SCRIPTURE: ....

PROMISE:

....
....

CIRCUMSTANCE:

....
....
....

RESPONSE:

....
....
....
....
....

DATE: .... SCRIPTURE: ....

PROMISE:

....

....

CIRCUMSTANCE:

....

....

....

RESPONSE:

....

....

....

....

....

DATE: .... SCRIPTURE: ....

PROMISE:

....

....

CIRCUMSTANCE:

....

....

....

RESPONSE:

....

....

....

....

....

DATE: ....   SCRIPTURE: ....

PROMISE:

....

....

CIRCUMSTANCE:

....

....

....

RESPONSE:

....

....

....

....

....

DATE: ....   SCRIPTURE: ....

PROMISE:

....

....

CIRCUMSTANCE:

....

....

....

RESPONSE:

....

....

....

....

....

DATE: ....   SCRIPTURE: ....

PROMISE:

....

....

CIRCUMSTANCE:

....

....

....

RESPONSE:

....

....

....

....

....

DATE: ....   SCRIPTURE: ....

PROMISE:

....

....

CIRCUMSTANCE:

....

....

....

RESPONSE:

....

....

....

....

....

DATE: .... SCRIPTURE: ....

PROMISE:

....
....

CIRCUMSTANCE:

....
....
....

RESPONSE:

....
....
....
....
....

DATE: .... SCRIPTURE: ....

PROMISE:

....
....

CIRCUMSTANCE:

....
....
....

RESPONSE:

....
....
....
....
....

DATE: ....   SCRIPTURE: ....

PROMISE:

....
....

CIRCUMSTANCE:

....
....
....

RESPONSE:

....
....
....
....
....

DATE: ....   SCRIPTURE: ....

PROMISE:

....
....

CIRCUMSTANCE:

....
....
....

RESPONSE:

....
....
....
....
....

DATE: ....   SCRIPTURE: ....

PROMISE:

....

....

CIRCUMSTANCE:

....

....

....

RESPONSE:

....

....

....

....

....

DATE: ....   SCRIPTURE: ....

PROMISE:

....

....

CIRCUMSTANCE:

....

....

....

RESPONSE:

....

....

....

....

....

DATE: ....   SCRIPTURE: ....

PROMISE:

....

....

CIRCUMSTANCE:

....

....

....

RESPONSE:

....

....

....

....

....

DATE: ....   SCRIPTURE: ....

PROMISE:

....

....

CIRCUMSTANCE:

....

....

....

RESPONSE:

....

....

....

....

....

DATE: .... SCRIPTURE: ....

PROMISE:

....
....

CIRCUMSTANCE:

....
....
....

RESPONSE:

....
....
....
....
....

DATE: .... SCRIPTURE: ....

PROMISE:

....
....

CIRCUMSTANCE:

....
....
....

RESPONSE:

....
....
....
....
....

DATE: ....   SCRIPTURE: ....

PROMISE:

....

....

CIRCUMSTANCE:

....

....

....

RESPONSE:

....

....

....

....

....

DATE: ....   SCRIPTURE: ....

PROMISE:

....

....

CIRCUMSTANCE:

....

....

....

RESPONSE:

....

....

....

....

....

DATE: .... SCRIPTURE: ....

PROMISE:

....

....

CIRCUMSTANCE:

....

....

....

RESPONSE:

....

....

....

....

....

DATE: .... SCRIPTURE: ....

PROMISE:

....

....

CIRCUMSTANCE:

....

....

....

RESPONSE:

....

....

....

....

....

DATE: ....   SCRIPTURE: ....

PROMISE:

....

....

CIRCUMSTANCE:

....

....

....

RESPONSE:

....

....

....

....

....

DATE: ....   SCRIPTURE: ....

PROMISE:

....

....

CIRCUMSTANCE:

....

....

....

RESPONSE:

....

....

....

....

....

DATE: ....   SCRIPTURE: ....

PROMISE:

....

....

CIRCUMSTANCE:

....

....

....

RESPONSE:

....

....

....

....

....

DATE: ....   SCRIPTURE: ....

PROMISE:

....

....

CIRCUMSTANCE:

....

....

....

RESPONSE:

....

....

....

....

....

DATE: .... SCRIPTURE: ....

PROMISE:

....

....

CIRCUMSTANCE:

....

....

....

RESPONSE:

....

....

....

....

....

DATE: .... SCRIPTURE: ....

PROMISE:

....

....

CIRCUMSTANCE:

....

....

....

RESPONSE:

....

....

....

....

....

DATE: .... SCRIPTURE: ....

PROMISE:

....
....

CIRCUMSTANCE:

....
....
....

RESPONSE:

....
....
....
....
....

DATE: .... SCRIPTURE: ....

PROMISE:

....
....

CIRCUMSTANCE:

....
....
....

RESPONSE:

....
....
....
....
....

DATE: ....   SCRIPTURE: ....

PROMISE:

....

....

CIRCUMSTANCE:

....

....

....

RESPONSE:

....

....

....

....

....

DATE: ....   SCRIPTURE: ....

PROMISE:

....

....

CIRCUMSTANCE:

....

....

....

RESPONSE:

....

....

....

....

....

DATE: .... SCRIPTURE:...............................

PROMISE:

....

....

CIRCUMSTANCE:

....

....

....

RESPONSE:

....

....

....

....

....

DATE: .... SCRIPTURE:...............................

PROMISE:

....

....

CIRCUMSTANCE:

....

....

....

RESPONSE:

....

....

....

....

....

DATE: .... SCRIPTURE: ....

PROMISE:

....

....

CIRCUMSTANCE:

....

....

....

RESPONSE:

....

....

....

....

....

DATE: .... SCRIPTURE: ....

PROMISE:

....

....

CIRCUMSTANCE:

....

....

....

RESPONSE:

....

....

....

....

....

DATE: ....   SCRIPTURE:.................................

PROMISE:

....

....

CIRCUMSTANCE:

....

....

....

RESPONSE:

....

....

....

....

....

DATE: ....   SCRIPTURE:.................................

PROMISE:

....

....

CIRCUMSTANCE:

....

....

....

RESPONSE:

....

....

....

....

....

DATE: .... SCRIPTURE: ....

PROMISE:

....
....

CIRCUMSTANCE:

....
....
....

RESPONSE:

....
....
....
....
....

DATE: .... SCRIPTURE: ....

PROMISE:

....
....

CIRCUMSTANCE:

....
....
....

RESPONSE:

....
....
....
....
....

DATE: .... SCRIPTURE: ....

PROMISE:

....

....

CIRCUMSTANCE:

....

....

....

RESPONSE:

....

....

....

....

....

DATE: .... SCRIPTURE: ....

PROMISE:

....

....

CIRCUMSTANCE:

....

....

....

RESPONSE:

....

....

....

....

....

DATE: ....   SCRIPTURE: ....

PROMISE:

....

....

CIRCUMSTANCE:

....

....

....

RESPONSE:

....

....

....

....

....

DATE: ....   SCRIPTURE: ....

PROMISE:

....

....

CIRCUMSTANCE:

....

....

....

RESPONSE:

....

....

....

....

....

DATE: .... SCRIPTURE: ....

PROMISE:

....

....

CIRCUMSTANCE:

....

....

....

RESPONSE:

....

....

....

....

....

DATE: .... SCRIPTURE: ....

PROMISE:

....

....

CIRCUMSTANCE:

....

....

....

RESPONSE:

....

....

....

....

....

DATE: ....   SCRIPTURE: ....

PROMISE:

....
....

CIRCUMSTANCE:

....
....
....

RESPONSE:

....
....
....
....
....

DATE: ....   SCRIPTURE: ....

PROMISE:

....
....

CIRCUMSTANCE:

....
....
....

RESPONSE:

....
....
....
....
....

DATE: .... SCRIPTURE: ....

PROMISE:

....

....

CIRCUMSTANCE:

....

....

....

RESPONSE:

....

....

....

....

....

DATE: .... SCRIPTURE: ....

PROMISE:

....

....

CIRCUMSTANCE:

....

....

....

RESPONSE:

....

....

....

....

....

DATE: ....   SCRIPTURE: ....

PROMISE:

....

....

CIRCUMSTANCE:

....

....

....

RESPONSE:

....

....

....

....

....

DATE: ....   SCRIPTURE: ....

PROMISE:

....

....

CIRCUMSTANCE:

....

....

....

RESPONSE:

....

....

....

....

....

DATE: .... SCRIPTURE: ....

PROMISE:

....
....

CIRCUMSTANCE:

....
....
....

RESPONSE:

....
....
....
....
....

DATE: .... SCRIPTURE: ....

PROMISE:

....
....

CIRCUMSTANCE:

....
....
....

RESPONSE:

....
....
....
....
....

DATE: .... SCRIPTURE: ....

PROMISE:

....

....

CIRCUMSTANCE:

....

....

....

RESPONSE:

....

....

....

....

....

DATE: .... SCRIPTURE: ....

PROMISE:

....

....

CIRCUMSTANCE:

....

....

....

RESPONSE:

....

....

....

....

....

DATE: ....   SCRIPTURE: ....

PROMISE:

....
....

CIRCUMSTANCE:

....
....
....

RESPONSE:

....
....
....
....
....

DATE: ....   SCRIPTURE: ....

PROMISE:

....
....

CIRCUMSTANCE:

....
....
....

RESPONSE:

....
....
....
....
....

DATE: .... SCRIPTURE: ....

PROMISE:

....

....

CIRCUMSTANCE:

....

....

....

RESPONSE:

....

....

....

....

....

DATE: .... SCRIPTURE: ....

PROMISE:

....

....

CIRCUMSTANCE:

....

....

....

RESPONSE:

....

....

....

....

....

DATE: .... SCRIPTURE: ....

PROMISE:

....

....

CIRCUMSTANCE:

....

....

....

RESPONSE:

....

....

....

....

....

DATE: .... SCRIPTURE: ....

PROMISE:

....

....

CIRCUMSTANCE:

....

....

....

RESPONSE:

....

....

....

....

....

DATE: ....   SCRIPTURE: ....

PROMISE:

....
....

CIRCUMSTANCE:

....
....
....

RESPONSE:

....
....
....
....
....

DATE: ....   SCRIPTURE: ....

PROMISE:

....
....

CIRCUMSTANCE:

....
....
....

RESPONSE:

....
....
....
....
....

DATE: ....   SCRIPTURE: ....

PROMISE:

....

....

CIRCUMSTANCE:

....

....

....

RESPONSE:

....

....

....

....

....

DATE: ....   SCRIPTURE: ....

PROMISE:

....

....

CIRCUMSTANCE:

....

....

....

RESPONSE:

....

....

....

....

....

DATE: ....   SCRIPTURE: ....

PROMISE:

....

....

CIRCUMSTANCE:

....

....

....

RESPONSE:

....

....

....

....

....

DATE: ....   SCRIPTURE: ....

PROMISE:

....

....

CIRCUMSTANCE:

....

....

....

RESPONSE:

....

....

....

....

....

DATE: .... SCRIPTURE: ....

PROMISE:

....

....

CIRCUMSTANCE:

....

....

....

RESPONSE:

....

....

....

....

....

DATE: .... SCRIPTURE: ....

PROMISE:

....

....

CIRCUMSTANCE:

....

....

....

RESPONSE:

....

....

....

....

....

DATE: .... SCRIPTURE: ....

PROMISE:

....

....

CIRCUMSTANCE:

....

....

....

RESPONSE:

....

....

....

....

....

DATE: .... SCRIPTURE: ....

PROMISE:

....

....

CIRCUMSTANCE:

....

....

....

RESPONSE:

....

....

....

....

....

DATE: .... SCRIPTURE: ....

PROMISE:

....

....

CIRCUMSTANCE:

....

....

....

RESPONSE:

....

....

....

....

....

DATE: .... SCRIPTURE: ....

PROMISE:

....

....

CIRCUMSTANCE:

....

....

....

RESPONSE:

....

....

....

....

....

DATE: ....   SCRIPTURE: ....

PROMISE:

....
....

CIRCUMSTANCE:

....
....
....

RESPONSE:

....
....
....
....
....

DATE: ....   SCRIPTURE: ....

PROMISE:

....
....

CIRCUMSTANCE:

....
....
....

RESPONSE:

....
....
....
....
....

DATE: ....   SCRIPTURE: ....

PROMISE:

....
....

CIRCUMSTANCE:

....
....
....

RESPONSE:

....
....
....
....
....

DATE: ....   SCRIPTURE: ....

PROMISE:

....
....

CIRCUMSTANCE:

....
....
....

RESPONSE:

....
....
....
....
....

DATE: ....   SCRIPTURE:................................

PROMISE:

....
....

CIRCUMSTANCE:

....
....
....

RESPONSE:

....
....
....
....
....

DATE: ....   SCRIPTURE:................................

PROMISE:

....
....

CIRCUMSTANCE:

....
....
....

RESPONSE:

....
....
....
....
....

DATE: .... SCRIPTURE: ....

PROMISE:

....

....

CIRCUMSTANCE:

....

....

....

RESPONSE:

....

....

....

....

....

DATE: .... SCRIPTURE: ....

PROMISE:

....

....

CIRCUMSTANCE:

....

....

....

RESPONSE:

....

....

....

....

....

DATE: .... SCRIPTURE: ....

PROMISE:

....
....

CIRCUMSTANCE:

....
....
....

RESPONSE:

....
....
....
....
....

DATE: .... SCRIPTURE: ....

PROMISE:

....
....

CIRCUMSTANCE:

....
....
....

RESPONSE:

....
....
....
....
....

DATE: .... SCRIPTURE: ....

PROMISE:

....
....

CIRCUMSTANCE:

....
....
....

RESPONSE:

....
....
....
....
....

DATE: .... SCRIPTURE: ....

PROMISE:

....
....

CIRCUMSTANCE:

....
....
....

RESPONSE:

....
....
....
....
....

DATE: .... SCRIPTURE: ....

PROMISE:

....

....

CIRCUMSTANCE:

....

....

....

RESPONSE:

....

....

....

....

....

DATE: .... SCRIPTURE: ....

PROMISE:

....

....

CIRCUMSTANCE:

....

....

....

RESPONSE:

....

....

....

....

....

DATE: .... SCRIPTURE: ....

PROMISE:

....
....

CIRCUMSTANCE:

....
....
....

RESPONSE:

....
....
....
....
....

DATE: .... SCRIPTURE: ....

PROMISE:

....
....

CIRCUMSTANCE:

....
....
....

RESPONSE:

....
....
....
....
....

DATE: .... SCRIPTURE: ....

PROMISE:

....

....

CIRCUMSTANCE:

....

....

....

RESPONSE:

....

....

....

....

....

DATE: .... SCRIPTURE: ....

PROMISE:

....

....

CIRCUMSTANCE:

....

....

....

RESPONSE:

....

....

....

....

....

DATE: ....   SCRIPTURE:...............................

PROMISE:

....
....

CIRCUMSTANCE:

....
....
....

RESPONSE:

....
....
....
....
....

DATE: ....   SCRIPTURE:...............................

PROMISE:

....
....

CIRCUMSTANCE:

....
....
....

RESPONSE:

....
....
....
....
....

DATE: .... SCRIPTURE: ....

PROMISE:

....

....

CIRCUMSTANCE:

....

....

....

RESPONSE:

....

....

....

....

....

DATE: .... SCRIPTURE: ....

PROMISE:

....

....

CIRCUMSTANCE:

....

....

....

RESPONSE:

....

....

....

....

....

DATE: ....   SCRIPTURE: ....

PROMISE:

....

....

CIRCUMSTANCE:

....

....

....

RESPONSE:

....

....

....

....

....

DATE: ....   SCRIPTURE: ....

PROMISE:

....

....

CIRCUMSTANCE:

....

....

....

RESPONSE:

....

....

....

....

....

DATE: .... SCRIPTURE: ....

PROMISE:

....

....

CIRCUMSTANCE:

....

....

....

RESPONSE:

....

....

....

....

....

DATE: .... SCRIPTURE: ....

PROMISE:

....

....

CIRCUMSTANCE:

....

....

....

RESPONSE:

....

....

....

....

....

DATE: ....   SCRIPTURE: ....

PROMISE:

....

....

CIRCUMSTANCE:

....

....

....

RESPONSE:

....

....

....

....

....

DATE: ....   SCRIPTURE: ....

PROMISE:

....

....

CIRCUMSTANCE:

....

....

....

RESPONSE:

....

....

....

....

....

DATE: .... SCRIPTURE: ....

PROMISE:

....

....

CIRCUMSTANCE:

....

....

....

RESPONSE:

....

....

....

....

....

DATE: .... SCRIPTURE: ....

PROMISE:

....

....

CIRCUMSTANCE:

....

....

....

RESPONSE:

....

....

....

....

....

DATE: ....   SCRIPTURE:................................

PROMISE:

....

....

CIRCUMSTANCE:

....

....

....

RESPONSE:

....

....

....

....

....

DATE: ....   SCRIPTURE:................................

PROMISE:

....

....

CIRCUMSTANCE:

....

....

....

RESPONSE:

....

....

....

....

....

DATE: .... SCRIPTURE: ....

PROMISE:

....

....

CIRCUMSTANCE:

....

....

....

RESPONSE:

....

....

....

....

....

DATE: .... SCRIPTURE: ....

PROMISE:

....

....

CIRCUMSTANCE:

....

....

....

RESPONSE:

....

....

....

....

....

DATE: ....   SCRIPTURE: ....

PROMISE:

....
....

CIRCUMSTANCE:

....
....
....

RESPONSE:

....
....
....
....
....

DATE: ....   SCRIPTURE: ....

PROMISE:

....
....

CIRCUMSTANCE:

....
....
....

RESPONSE:

....
....
....
....
....

DATE: .... SCRIPTURE: ....

PROMISE:

....

....

CIRCUMSTANCE:

....

....

....

RESPONSE:

....

....

....

....

....

DATE: .... SCRIPTURE: ....

PROMISE:

....

....

CIRCUMSTANCE:

....

....

....

RESPONSE:

....

....

....

....

....

DATE: ....   SCRIPTURE: ....

PROMISE:

....

....

CIRCUMSTANCE:

....

....

....

RESPONSE:

....

....

....

....

....

DATE: ....   SCRIPTURE: ....

PROMISE:

....

....

CIRCUMSTANCE:

....

....

....

RESPONSE:

....

....

....

....

....

DATE: .... SCRIPTURE: ....

PROMISE:

....
....

CIRCUMSTANCE:

....
....
....

RESPONSE:

....
....
....
....
....

DATE: .... SCRIPTURE: ....

PROMISE:

....
....

CIRCUMSTANCE:

....
....
....

RESPONSE:

....
....
....
....
....

DATE: ....   SCRIPTURE: ....

PROMISE:

....
....

CIRCUMSTANCE:

....
....
....

RESPONSE:

....
....
....
....
....

DATE: ....   SCRIPTURE: ....

PROMISE:

....
....

CIRCUMSTANCE:

....
....
....

RESPONSE:

....
....
....
....
....

DATE: ....   SCRIPTURE: ....

PROMISE:

....
....

CIRCUMSTANCE:

....
....
....

RESPONSE:

....
....
....
....
....

DATE: ....   SCRIPTURE: ....

PROMISE:

....
....

CIRCUMSTANCE:

....
....
....

RESPONSE:

....
....
....
....
....

DATE: .... SCRIPTURE: ....

PROMISE:

....

....

CIRCUMSTANCE:

....

....

....

RESPONSE:

....

....

....

....

....

DATE: .... SCRIPTURE: ....

PROMISE:

....

....

CIRCUMSTANCE:

....

....

....

RESPONSE:

....

....

....

....

....

DATE: ....   SCRIPTURE: ....

PROMISE:
....
....

CIRCUMSTANCE:
....
....
....

RESPONSE:
....
....
....
....
....

DATE: ....   SCRIPTURE: ....

PROMISE:
....
....

CIRCUMSTANCE:
....
....
....

RESPONSE:
....
....
....
....
....

DATE: .... SCRIPTURE: ....

PROMISE:

....

....

CIRCUMSTANCE:

....

....

....

RESPONSE:

....

....

....

....

....

DATE: .... SCRIPTURE: ....

PROMISE:

....

....

CIRCUMSTANCE:

....

....

....

RESPONSE:

....

....

....

....

....

DATE: .... SCRIPTURE: ....

PROMISE:

....

....

CIRCUMSTANCE:

....

....

....

RESPONSE:

....

....

....

....

....

DATE: .... SCRIPTURE: ....

PROMISE:

....

....

CIRCUMSTANCE:

....

....

....

RESPONSE:

....

....

....

....

....

DATE: ....   SCRIPTURE:................................

PROMISE:

....
....

CIRCUMSTANCE:

....
....
....

RESPONSE:

....
....
....
....
....

DATE: ....   SCRIPTURE:................................

PROMISE:

....
....

CIRCUMSTANCE:

....
....
....

RESPONSE:

....
....
....
....
....

DATE: .... SCRIPTURE: ....

PROMISE:

....
....

CIRCUMSTANCE:

....
....
....

RESPONSE:

....
....
....
....
....

DATE: .... SCRIPTURE: ....

PROMISE:

....
....

CIRCUMSTANCE:

....
....
....

RESPONSE:

....
....
....
....
....

DATE: .... SCRIPTURE: ....

PROMISE:

....

....

CIRCUMSTANCE:

....

....

....

RESPONSE:

....

....

....

....

....

DATE: .... SCRIPTURE: ....

PROMISE:

....

....

CIRCUMSTANCE:

....

....

....

RESPONSE:

....

....

....

....

....

DATE: .... SCRIPTURE: ....

PROMISE:

....

....

CIRCUMSTANCE:

....

....

....

RESPONSE:

....

....

....

....

....

DATE: .... SCRIPTURE: ....

PROMISE:

....

....

CIRCUMSTANCE:

....

....

....

RESPONSE:

....

....

....

....

....

DATE: .... SCRIPTURE: ....

PROMISE:

....
....

CIRCUMSTANCE:

....
....
....

RESPONSE:

....
....
....
....
....

DATE: .... SCRIPTURE: ....

PROMISE:

....
....

CIRCUMSTANCE:

....
....
....

RESPONSE:

....
....
....
....
....

DATE: ....   SCRIPTURE: ....

PROMISE:

....
....

CIRCUMSTANCE:

....
....
....

RESPONSE:

....
....
....
....
....

DATE: ....   SCRIPTURE: ....

PROMISE:

....
....

CIRCUMSTANCE:

....
....
....

RESPONSE:

....
....
....
....
....

DATE: ....   SCRIPTURE: ....

PROMISE:

....

....

CIRCUMSTANCE:

....

....

....

RESPONSE:

....

....

....

....

....

DATE: ....   SCRIPTURE: ....

PROMISE:

....

....

CIRCUMSTANCE:

....

....

....

RESPONSE:

....

....

....

....

....

DATE: .... SCRIPTURE: ....

PROMISE:

....

....

CIRCUMSTANCE:

....

....

....

RESPONSE:

....

....

....

....

....

DATE: .... SCRIPTURE: ....

PROMISE:

....

....

CIRCUMSTANCE:

....

....

....

RESPONSE:

....

....

....

....

....

DATE: .... SCRIPTURE: ....

PROMISE:

....

....

CIRCUMSTANCE:

....

....

....

RESPONSE:

....

....

....

....

....

DATE: .... SCRIPTURE: ....

PROMISE:

....

....

CIRCUMSTANCE:

....

....

....

RESPONSE:

....

....

....

....

....

DATE: .... SCRIPTURE: ....

PROMISE:

....

....

CIRCUMSTANCE:

....

....

....

RESPONSE:

....

....

....

....

....

DATE: .... SCRIPTURE: ....

PROMISE:

....

....

CIRCUMSTANCE:

....

....

....

RESPONSE:

....

....

....

....

....

DATE: ....   SCRIPTURE: ....

PROMISE:

....

....

CIRCUMSTANCE:

....

....

....

RESPONSE:

....

....

....

....

....

DATE: ....   SCRIPTURE: ....

PROMISE:

....

....

CIRCUMSTANCE:

....

....

....

RESPONSE:

....

....

....

....

....

DATE: .... SCRIPTURE: ....

PROMISE:

....

....

CIRCUMSTANCE:

....

....

....

RESPONSE:

....

....

....

....

....

DATE: .... SCRIPTURE: ....

PROMISE:

....

....

CIRCUMSTANCE:

....

....

....

RESPONSE:

....

....

....

....

....

DATE: .... SCRIPTURE: ....

PROMISE:

....
....

CIRCUMSTANCE:

....
....
....

RESPONSE:

....
....
....
....
....

DATE: .... SCRIPTURE: ....

PROMISE:

....
....

CIRCUMSTANCE:

....
....
....

RESPONSE:

....
....
....
....
....

DATE: .... SCRIPTURE: ....

PROMISE:

....

....

CIRCUMSTANCE:

....

....

....

RESPONSE:

....

....

....

....

....

DATE: .... SCRIPTURE: ....

PROMISE:

....

....

CIRCUMSTANCE:

....

....

....

RESPONSE:

....

....

....

....

....

DATE: ....   SCRIPTURE: ....

PROMISE:

....

....

CIRCUMSTANCE:

....

....

....

RESPONSE:

....

....

....

....

....

DATE: ....   SCRIPTURE: ....

PROMISE:

....

....

CIRCUMSTANCE:

....

....

....

RESPONSE:

....

....

....

....

....

DATE: ....   SCRIPTURE: ....

PROMISE:

....
....

CIRCUMSTANCE:

....
....
....

RESPONSE:

....
....
....
....
....

DATE: ....   SCRIPTURE: ....

PROMISE:

....
....

CIRCUMSTANCE:

....
....
....

RESPONSE:

....
....
....
....
....

DATE: .... SCRIPTURE: ....

PROMISE:

....

....

CIRCUMSTANCE:

....

....

....

RESPONSE:

....

....

....

....

....

DATE: .... SCRIPTURE: ....

PROMISE:

....

....

CIRCUMSTANCE:

....

....

....

RESPONSE:

....

....

....

....

....

DATE: ....   SCRIPTURE: ....

PROMISE:

....

....

CIRCUMSTANCE:

....

....

....

RESPONSE:

....

....

....

....

....

DATE: ....   SCRIPTURE: ....

PROMISE:

....

....

CIRCUMSTANCE:

....

....

....

RESPONSE:

....

....

....

....

....

DATE: .... SCRIPTURE: ....

PROMISE:

....

....

CIRCUMSTANCE:

....

....

....

RESPONSE:

....

....

....

....

....

DATE: .... SCRIPTURE: ....

PROMISE:

....

....

CIRCUMSTANCE:

....

....

....

RESPONSE:

....

....

....

....

....

DATE: .... SCRIPTURE: ....

PROMISE:

....

....

CIRCUMSTANCE:

....

....

....

RESPONSE:

....

....

....

....

....

DATE: .... SCRIPTURE: ....

PROMISE:

....

....

CIRCUMSTANCE:

....

....

....

RESPONSE:

....

....

....

....

....